THE PERFECT STORM

PATRICK BET-DAVID

Author of *The 25 Laws for Doing the Impossible*

Acknowledgments

Let me start off by acknowledging how fortunate I am to have met my wife Jennifer, who is the best thing that ever happened to me. It takes a very special woman to marry a man like me, and God hand-selected her to be right next to me as we go on this journey called Life. I thank God every day for giving me a wife like her.

I want to thank my parents Diana and Gabreal, who had the courage to escape the war-stricken environment of Iran to bring us to the land of all opportunities. It was an interesting journey of getting here, but it was all worth it. It's a responsibility of mine to represent my bloodline in a way that makes both of my parents proud.

If there's a man I can call my hero, it would be Gabreal Bet-David. It's a rare thing nowadays to have a father who isn't concerned about pleasing you all the time because he knows that he's responsible for raising a man who can stand on his own after he's gone. My father has done exactly that. Anyone who has ever met my dad will tell you that spending an hour with him isn't enough; you want him around all the time. His wisdom is priceless.

I have to thank two of the greatest listeners in the world, who are willing to sit there and listen to me as I bounce ideas off of them for hours. I rarely get any response back from them, but just the fact that they listen makes a world of difference. I'm sure my two little Shih Tzu dogs will be thrilled as they read this acknowledgment of their efforts over the years.

I'd like to thank many of my friends all over the country who took the time to read the manuscript while it was going through its different stages of development. Your honest feedback was invaluable.

Last but not least I'd like to thank all of those who have challenged and inspired me over the years in all areas of my life: Kim Sinclair, my health and guidance teacher in high school, who inspired me to join the army; Drill Sergeant Green, who pushed me to a limit I had never been pushed to before in boot camp; all of my army buddies from the 326ENG Battalion in Fort Campbell (I would need a whole book to share the stories we experienced together); Bradford, Guttierez, Aghakianest, and McLroy, who all were crazy in their own way and helped make the experience extremely entertaining; Dave Kirby, who gave me the opportunity to start my career in the financial industry at twenty-one years old at Morgan Stanley without having a college degree, which was a requirement; Bill Vogel, who invited me to a special event in March 2009 where George Will was the keynote speaker, who in turn inspired the "Saving America" crusade; my sister Polet Bet-David, whom I love dearly (I learn every day from the incredible example she sets of being a mother to my two little best friends, Grace and Sean); and my brother-in-law, Siamak Sabetimani, who I believe is a saint. Thank you additionally to all the leaders in PHP who decided to embark on the great awakening of "Saving America" at a time when all the odds were against us. I admire your excellence in building unity, all while having a touch of madness and a spoonful of competition combined with a sprinkle of craziness. You inspire me more than words can describe. Thanks as well to Pastor Dudley Rutherford, who constantly was in my ear while I was making some of the most important decisions of my life.

I especially want to thank our competitors and critics, who remind me on a daily basis that I'm still alive; the day that they stop, life stops. Thank you for your efforts.

Let's go make history.

Contents

Statement of Purpose

"It's getting late. Time is running out."

Only God knows how many times I've said this phrase, but I can't take credit for this statement. My father, Gabreal Bet-David, constantly reminded me that the clock is ticking and that life will pass you by in no time. I've come to realize that in all aspects of our lives there will come a time when we must rise up and take advantage of the opportunity that lies ahead of us. The challenge with us as human beings is that we tend to think we have plenty of time to get our things in order, until we realize it's too late. I'm coming to you from a place of having personally experienced this myself.

I want to encourage you to read this book with an open mind, but at the same time I challenge you to verify the validity of the timing that exists in a specific sector of the financial services industry mentioned in the book. I would certainly suggest you do so before it's too late and the time has passed you by. There will be a short window of opportunity with how perfect the current conditions are, but I want you to judge this for yourself. By the time you're done reading the book, you will have a clear understanding of how the different conditions have come together to create *The Next Perfect Storm.*

Introduction

June 20th, 1999, was a day filled with mixed feelings of joy and uncertainty. After my last day of being stationed with the 101st Airborne Division in Fort Campbell, Kentucky, I was on a flight back home wondering what I would be doing next. What civilian job would be a right fit for someone with shooting expertise with an M-16 from 300 meters away, who could additionally rappel out of a helicopter and was the best hummer mechanic in our unit? I couldn't forget mentioning in my resume that I could do eighty-two push-ups non-stop in two minutes. Can you imagine the look on an employer's face when I would list my qualifications?

Knowing the unique nature of my resume, I decided to get a job in a field I was very familiar with. I took a job at the Bally Total Fitness in Culver City, California, while going to school part time. It was a good job, one that suited my physical skills, but it was not something that I could do for the rest of my life.

While working at the gym, I had a chance to meet many different people from all walks of life. I was always curious to know why some of the people I met earned over $300,000 a year while others were only making $60,000 a year. Both income groups consisted of quality people who were willing to work hard, so why such a big gap in their yearly pay? Initially I assumed that the high-income earners all had a four-year or an eight-year degree, but I found out this wasn't the case. In both categories I met people who had degrees and others who didn't.

The next thing I started asking while selling gym memberships was how my customers liked their work and how it impacted their personal lives. I grew up in an environment where the stereotype about rich people was they didn't have a personal life. All they cared about was money, and the rest of their lives didn't matter. But the more time I spent asking questions, the more I realized that in all income brackets there were people who had good personal lives and others who didn't. Some of the top income earners were involved in industries that required them to work seven days a week, which seriously affected their personal lives. I also noticed that those who earned around $60,000 a year had a hard time supporting their families financially, which created a lot of familial hardships that in many cases led to divorce.

These answers only created more questions for me. I was inspired to search for an industry that provided the opportunity to earn a great living while having a great personal life. I wanted to be able to provide for my future family while simultaneously getting to spend quality time with them. After all, without a great family life, what's the point of a high income?

This was a severely challenging time in my own life financially and emotionally. My father's health was declining, which caused him to have several heart attacks. During that same time I ended up accumulating $49,000 of credit card debt on twenty-six different credit cards. It was very annoying dealing with the creditors who were calling me every single day to collect debt. I thought about money all day. I mentioned the stereotype that all rich people think about is money; this is how I felt, but the difference was that I had no money. Even so, money was all I thought about.

> "A single conversation across the table with a wise man is worth a month's study of books."
>
> — Chinese Proverb

I attended a seminar in 2000 where I met a gentleman named Bob who challenged my way of financial thinking in a way that no person ever had done before. Bob was a speaker at this seminar, and after he delivered a great message I asked him for his card so we could stay in contact with each other. A few days later I went to lunch with him, where I got a chance to get to know him better. I asked him many questions about money, but he kept changing the subject. Finally he stopped me and asked, "Son, do you know why all you think about is money?" I replied, "No, tell me." He asked, "What would be the first thing you would be thinking about if I were to cover your nose and your mouth?" I had no idea where he was going with this, but I answered, "Air." He asked me why, so I gave the obvious answer: "Because I wouldn't have any of it." He followed this with what struck me as a weird question, asking, "Do you ever catch yourself walking around bragging about how much air you have?" At this point, I started questioning whether it was coffee he was drinking or hard liquor. What kind of a question was that? Simply curious to know where he was going with this, I replied, "No, that would be stupid." He immediately said, "It would be stupid because when you have plenty of air to breathe the last thing you're thinking about is the amount of oxygen you have at your disposal. That's exactly how money works. Do you know why all you think about is money?" Again, I said, "No, tell me." "Because you have none of it," he revealed. "When you have plenty of money, the last thing you think about is money. Your mind becomes free to start thinking about things that actually have meaning in life. The key is to get the money issue solved as quickly as possible so you can start having the freedom to do the things you were really put on this planet to do."

I wasn't happy with the answer, but he was absolutely right. I had many great ideas on what I wanted to do in life, but when your mind is consumed by your financial problems, you minimize the time and energy you have to think about the bigger picture.

This exchange challenged my way of thinking and inspired a sense of urgency to learn how money works. I was anxious to get that issue resolved as quickly as possible so that I could have the freedom to do the things I'd always dreamt of doing. I'm a firm believer that every one of us wants that as well, for ourselves and our families. We all want to put our mark on this universe before we leave it.

Before I get into the topic of what's the next boom, it's very important for me to clarify why I decided to write this book. I've had the privilege of meeting thousands of people over the last ten years, and I'm always amazed at how many people with unique, God-given abilities never get a chance to live their life to its full potential. Often times the reason for that is that they spend their entire life concerned about solving financial problems, which keeps them distracted from why they're here. The purpose of this book is to show you that there is an industry that is currently experiencing a "perfect storm" that could give you the opportunity of becoming financially independent while simultaneously having a personal life. In reading this book, your mindset will be challenged numerous times and many of the conditions that you've been brought up accepting will be questioned.

In order for an industry to experience a perfect storm, there needs to be a combination of several different conditions that generates a certain level of intensity, momentum, and power in that industry. Individuals can't create this kind of power on their own; but if they take advantage of it when the conditions are just right, they have the potential to be phenomenally successful. It's a rarity to see a perfect storm occur, but ultra-successful businessmen and women who you read about have generally been involved in one. The perfect storm makes the average person seem like they belong in the movie *The Avengers*. The key is to time the storm accurately while having the courage to get involved in the industry and put your energy and dedication into it. Knowing about the next perfect storm means absolutely nothing if no action is taken. You can be knowledgeable about the different conditions that make up the perfect storm, but if you don't act you won't reap the benefits of it.

On a Saturday afternoon in 2001, I was invited to go to Newport Beach to meet a few people. Little did I know that this was a day that I would never forget for the rest of my life! We don't have too many of those days, but this was sure one of them. The meeting was held on a yacht at the Balboa Bay Club, where I knew in advance that some of the people I was going to meet were very well off financially. When we got there we were greeted by cocktail waitresses who offered us a choice of red or white wine and hors d'oeuvres. This was certainly new to me, considering the chow hall in the army never gave us this kind of service.

After a few minutes of meeting and greeting others, I was introduced to a gentleman named Robert who owned the yacht and many others next to it. At this point I was starting to feel a little more comfortable with the crowd and figured that this could be my opportunity to ask Robert questions about business and different industries. He had enough charisma to fill an entire football stadium, with a sense of humor that made me like him instantly. He was certainly sarcastic, but the kind of sarcastic that wasn't hateful. He was a man with so many life experiences who knew how to captivate the entire audience with his style of storytelling.

I only got a chance to ask one central question, as it led to a long session of him speaking while I just listened. It was like a scene out of the movies when someone with a lot of influence speaks. A crowd quickly gathered around us to hear what Robert had to say.

Here is what I asked: "Is there an industry that gives you the opportunity to make as much money as you'd like while having a life as well?"

He gave me this grin and with no hesitation asked me, "What are the busiest days of the week?" I replied, "Either the beginning of the week, or the end of the week." He nodded his head in agreement but asked, "What would most Americans like to do on a Friday morning?" I could only speak for myself, and because I worked on Friday mornings I said, "It would be kind of nice to be able to spend the time relaxing with the family, maybe going to the beach." He immediately said, "Most rich people in America would like to be at the country club golfing on Friday morning."

This is where he lost me for a minute. Being born in Iran, the last thing we do on Friday morning is go golfing; we kind of prefer to stay away from bunkers (you golfers out there will understand the joke). But not wanting to get off topic, I asked, "What does this have to do with my question?" "The majority of the people who golf on Friday morning are in the insurance industry," Robert said. "They get involved in the industry and after five, ten, or fifteen years they build themselves a book of business that generates them a stream of income, which eventually allows them to do what they would like to do. And one of those things is golfing."

Now keep in mind that this is happening in 2001 and many people in California were talking about getting involved in real estate, including myself. This led me to my next question: "How about the real estate industry?" It didn't take me a long time to realize that his responses were very direct. He wasn't too concerned about being politically correct. "Patrick, you said you were looking for an industry that will allow you to make a lot of money but also have a life, right? I have many friends in real estate who have made millions of dollars, however that came with a sacrifice. Here are the numbers for you to keep in mind. For every ten years in real estate, you have a divorce. For every three months in real estate, you lose a month of your life. The highs are too high and the lows are too low, which puts way too much pressure on your personal life. And unlike insurance, the longer you are in the real estate industry, the more of your time it demands. I am a big supporter of investing in real estate, but don't recommend it as a career. So if you're planning on staying single and just marrying your career, then real estate is not a bad choice—but you said you wanted to have a life as well."

I was very surprised by his answer, but I couldn't argue with it. I had personally seen with my own eyes what happened to many of my relatives and friends who got involved in the real estate industry. But I still wasn't fully clear why he recommended the insurance industry, so I asked him to explain his reasons. He answered, "Whether you look to your left or to your right, your car, your jewelry, your cell phone, your life, your bank, and your government are all backed up by insurance companies. The reason for that is because insurance companies have some of the deepest pockets." But I still fully didn't get it and looked a little puzzled, which prompted him to ask this question: "What are the richest sports in America?" Now I'm 6'5" and 240 pounds, and I've played sports all of my life, so I replied, "Baseball and basketball." But Robert countered, "Baseball and basketball are the poor man's sports." Offended and confused, I asked, "Why?" "Not because the players and the teams don't make money," he said. "All you need to do is pay attention to the commercials that are aired during those games. You normally see commercials for Budweiser, Nike, Coca Cola, or McDonald's, and the reason for that is because that's what middle America buys." I gave him a frustrated look, thinking to myself that that's exactly what I buy. But his words finally clicked when he finished with this: "Patrick, the richest sports in the world are golf and tennis. Have you ever paid attention to the kind of companies that advertise and sponsor those tournaments? Life insurance companies, such as ING, Allianz, Hartford, All-State, Prudential, Pacific Life—the list goes on. The reason for that is the wealthy individuals in America understand how life insurance works while the majority of people don't. Before it's too late, learn about how money and insurance work."

> "There's nothing better when something comes and hits you and you think 'YES!'"
>
> — J.K. Rowling

That epiphanic moment is what influenced me to consider a career in the financial services industry. The only concern for me was whether I could be successful or not, since my background had nothing to do with the financial services industry. But no matter how many times I tried to convince myself to discredit all the reasons I'd heard, I knew that my family was counting on me to deliver.

Being a rookie in the financial services industry, I decided to start applying to some of the largest financial firms in America. On a drive back from watching Ronnie Coleman win the 2001 Mr. Olympia contest in Las Vegas, I got a call from Mr. Kirby offering me a position with Morgan Stanley Dean Witter as a financial advisor. I was thrilled about the opportunity. Monday, September 10th, 2001, was my first day of work at Morgan Stanley. I was going through my onboarding process, which involved a three-week trip to the Morgan Stanley headquarters at the World Trade Center. The next day was September 11th, a day no one will ever forget. We were having a meeting early in the morning with our manager when one of the brokers screamed out from his desk, "Turn on the TV, turn on the TV!!!" We watched the second plane hit the World Trade Center while the newscaster fell into stunned silence. Everything changed that day. I remember us running out of the building to go home to our families. The following day the market tanked and the calls were coming in at a feverish pace from clients wanting to know what they could do to stop the bleeding. I saw the look on many of the stockbrokers' faces who didn't want to take clients' calls because they had no answers. No one had the answer! At the close of business, Mr. Kirby brought us all together and gave us a talk that was very direct and honest. He told us that the next few years were going to be some of the most difficult times to be a financial advisor. He admitted that he didn't have all the answers and that he understood that people were going to walk away from the industry, but he challenged us to keep serving the client. And that's how I started my career in the financial industry.

I have now been in the financial industry for over a decade and I have never seen the business conditions as good as they are today. It's this particular set of conditions that creates a perfect storm today. Over the next few chapters I will be making several points on why this is one of the industries that will be flourishing over the next decade, and each point will validate the argument. I'm here to give you the facts and let you decide for yourself what to do with them. But there is one thing I am certain of: The majority of people will miss this boom, and I want to challenge you to be part of the minority instead of the majority.

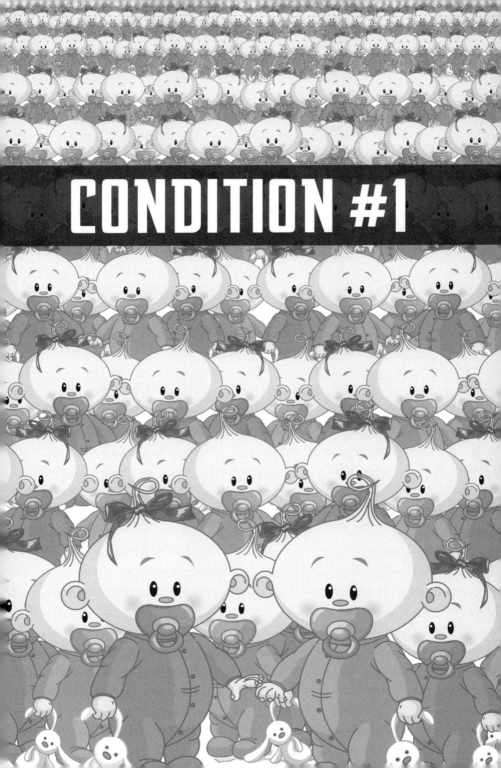

CONDITION #1

CONDITION #1
OF THE PERFECT STORM:

—— Baby Boomer Phenomenon ——

> "The two most important requirements for major success are: first, being in the right place at the right time, and second, doing something about it."
>
> — Ray Crock

Would you agree that the success of a business has a lot to do with timing? Throughout history timing has been a major cause of many Americans' wealth. If you think about the '90s, what industry would you say created the most millionaires? Do you remember what happened in Silicon Valley? It seemed like every other day a new company was experiencing a level of growth that caused their stock to double over and over again. But even with these amazing statistics, would you say that most people started investing in the stock market early on in the boom, or did they wait until 1999? Most people waited until 1999 to invest, but by then it was too late. The next boom was experienced somewhere between 2000 and 2007, and that was the real estate boom. Again the question is, did most people get involved in real estate in the early 2000s, or did we wait until '04 or '05? Once again, the vast majority invested too late to experience the surge of the boom.

I've finally come to the conclusion that human nature has a tendency to want to wait and see if others experience success first before diving in ourselves, but by then, the opportunity has more than likely passed us by. Have you ever caught yourself telling a friend, "Why don't you go make money first, then call me?" By the time he calls you it's too late. Pay very close attention to the details in the next few chapters, especially if you missed the last two booms; you certainly don't want to miss this next one.

It's been said that if you want to time the market and make a fortune, find out what Baby Boomers need next and do something about it at the early stages of the boom. If you look at the Baby Boomer generation you will see an interesting trend: An estimated 76 million Baby Boomers were born in America from 1946 to 1964. That may not compare to the numbers in China or India, but there's never been a time when more babies were born in America. But the question you may ask is, why were they born after 1946? World War II ended in 1945, which allowed many soldiers to return to their families. What would you say was on the top of a soldier's list when he saw the wife he hadn't seen for a while? You got it: making babies. America was on fire making babies during that eighteen year period.

I want you to imagine that today is 1946, and that you know that in the next eighteen years 76 million babies are going to be born. What industry would you get involved in that offers products for babies? You're probably thinking baby food, toys, baby shampoo, etc. What companies come to mind when you think about those products? Gerber, Mattel, Johnson & Johnson? All three of them experienced an unprecedented surge in their business during this time. As a matter of fact, Mattel was founded in 1945 by Harold Matson and Elliot Handler, the year that World War II came to an end. Does that tell you anything about timing? How about Barbie? When do you think Mattel came out with Barbie? On March 9th, 1959, Barbie was founded and ended up being a toy sold worldwide, all because of the boom taking place in America. I don't want to discard the strategic advertising and marketing that Mattel had in place, but they absolutely capitalized on the timing.

Let's consider the different booms that have occurred since the birth of the Baby Boomer generation:

1950s:

In the '50s and early '60s, Boomers started turning five to seven years old. What do kids start attending at that age? Schools. But there was a challenge with the number of Boomers needing to go to school, considering there weren't enough schools to facilitate 76 million children. There was a need to build more schools. Which industry do you think boomed next? Since there was a need to develop schools, the construction industry started booming. The U.S. Department of Education did a study in January of 1999 titled "How Old Are America's Public Schools?" Here's how the numbers broke down:

28% of all public schools were built in America before 1950s

45% from 1950 to 1969

17% from 1970 to 1984

10% from 1985 to 1999

"The increase in the construction of schools between 1950 and 1969 corresponds to the years during which the Baby Boomer generation was going to school."

— National Center for Education Statistics

1960s to 1970s:

The next phase was another big boom that took place in America. In the '60s and '70s, Baby Boomers started turning sixteen years old. What gift would you say most sixteen year olds would like to receive for their birthday? You've got it: a car. There was a major boom in the automobile industry in the '60s. What cars do you think experienced a boom during that time because of the perfect timing?

Dodge Charger 1964	
Ford Mustang 1964	
Pontiac GTO 1964	
Chevrolet Camaro 1966	
Pontiac Firebird 1967	

If you mention any of these cars to Baby Boomers, you may have them tell you a story about their first car.

1970s to 1980s:

This is when Boomers started turning thirty years old. The next phase of life had arrived. It was about settling down and having a family. The next step was becom-  ing a home owner and achieving the American Dream. We experienced a real estate boom in the late 1970s, as well as the late '80s because of the Baby Boomers. The real estate market gave a return of 8.12% during that decade.

Late 1980s and the 1990s:

This was the era of accumulating wealth. It was no longer just about buying real estate, but about really diversifying their assets to increase their net worth. They start-

ed paying attention to returns on their portfolio. This is when mutual funds started becoming very attractive to Baby Boomers. Mutual funds and stocks started booming.

2010 to 2030:

It is April of 2012 as I write this book. Baby Boomers today are between the ages of forty-eight and sixty-six years old. What do you think is on Boomers' minds? Retirement! One in four Amer-

icans is a Baby Boomer. This is the largest population group in U.S. history. A Baby Boomer turns fifty every eighteen seconds and sixty every seven seconds. They're no longer thinking about the next penny stock or the next hot mutual fund. Whether they're sixty-six years old or forty-eight, they are thinking about retirement.

For decades, retirement meant giving thirty years of your life to a company in trade for a pension plan that takes care of you for the rest of your life. Those days are slowly but surely drifting away. According to the IRS, the number of pension plans available has dropped from around 114,000 in 1985 to around 38,000 in 2010. Which direction do you think these numbers are headed toward by 2030 or 2050? These are loyal individuals who have followed the system to the tee and are now concerned whether their savings will last through their lifetime, or will it run out?

The 401k plan was introduced in 1978 to supplement your income from your pension plan during retirement, but for many the plan didn't produce the results people were expecting to get. *Time Magazine* did an article on October 9th, 2009, titled "Why It's Time to Retire the 401k," in which they showed the performance of the plan from 1998 to 2008. According to the study, the average 401k account had $47,004 in 1998. Imagine if it's 1998 and your statement on your 401k reads roughly $47,000? Where would you expect the amount to be ten years later in 2008? Most people would probably be happy if it doubled, or gave a return of 6 to 8%, but the real account balance by 2008 was a whopping $45,519. That means in ten years the average 401k account lost $1,485. How many Baby Boomers do you think can afford another decade like the last one? What most of them are looking for is an investment vehicle that will give them the highest possible return with the lowest amount of risk.

Time Magazine Oct. 19, 2009

Average 401k balance in 1998:	**$47,004**
Average 401k balance in 2008:	**$45,519**
Ten year total change in value:	**($1,485)**

An annuity becomes a great fit for many of these Boomers. Annuities got a black eye from the '80s through the 2000s because their returns couldn't compare to the returns in the stock market, or real estate market. But after what took place at the end of the tech boom, 9/11, and the real estate boom, more Boomers are becoming interested in annuities. The simplest explanation of annuities is an investment vehicle issued by insurance companies primarily to provide income during retirement. They come with a number of different options that can be tailored to fit an investor's cash flow and future income needs. This is why you're starting to see more and more Baby Boomers requesting to find out more information about annuities. Although annuities may not be for everyone, they sure fit like a perfect glove for many Boomers. The internet has made it easy for Boomers to have access to information; they are now more educated about money than ever before, and annuities are one of the vehicles in particular they are interested in. The desire for Boomers to look at annuities as an option will be going on for the next two decades. And therein lies a phenomenal opportunity.

The following graph shows the returns on investing $100,000 in an account such as a CD with a return of 3%, in the S&P 500, or an indexed annuity from 1998 to 2011. These results are certainly not an indication that they will beat the S&P every time. They simply demonstrate the effectiveness of annuities in years when the S&P 500 was negative.

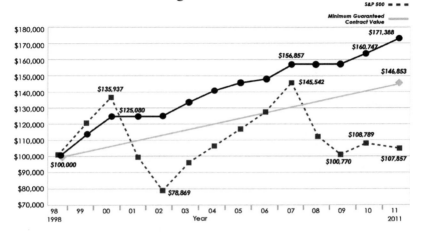

Annuities have a longer history than most investment vehicles. They were initially called "annua," a term which was used by the Roman Empire to recognize their loyal soldiers. They are used in so many different places, but they are not always labeled as annuities. For instance, most pension plans that are offered to employees who give twenty, or thirty years of their lives to the companies are, in fact, annuities. Many teachers, firefighters, police officers, military personnel, and government employees have their retirement paid to them in the form of an annuity. The State lotto system uses an annuity to make payments over the course of twenty years to lottery winners. The legendary baseball player Babe Ruth survived the infamous stock market crash of 1929 thanks to annuities; advised by his mentor and sports cartoonist Christy Walsh, Ruth put his money into annuities before the crash. Due to that decision, Babe Ruth was financially secure during the Great Depression, while many celebrities had to start all over again. Last but not least, Benjamin Franklin was an early supporter of the concept of annuities. At his death in 1790, he left in his will two annuities to the cities of Philadelphia and Boston.

WHAT

An annuity is an investment that you make through an insurance company that provides tax-deferred growth, guarantees, safety, death benefit, flexibility, and the option of having a monthly stream of income that you cannot outlive.

WHEN   ONE OF THE OLDEST INSTRUMENTS

Mutual Funds	CDs	Annuities
1774 AD[1]	1,600 AD[2]	2,000 BC[3]

WHO

- Ben Franklin[6]
- Babe Ruth[5]

- State lottery system[4]
- Romans[7]

Benjamin Franklin was an early supporter of the concept of annuities and in his will left two annuities to the cities of Philadelphia and Boston. The Boston annuity lasted until 1993 when the city officials voted to end the annuity and use the lump sum that remained.

"I may take risks in life, but I will never risk my money, I use annuities and I never have to worry about my money." — Babe Ruth

The Boston annuity lasted over two hundred years, until the city officials voted to end the annuity in 1993 and use the lump sum that remained. I can go on and on with stories, but the point is

that Boomers have a tremendous need when it comes to making better decisions during their retirement years. This in turn has caused a tremendous demand in the life insurance and financial industries.

I want you to keep in mind that I've been in the industry for over a decade, having held licenses such as Series 7, 66, 31, 26, and Life and Health. I've had the opportunity to serve my clients in many different ways. After being involved in one way, or another in serving tens of thousands of families, I have come to the conclusion that no single product is perfect for everyone. I've sold both term and permanent policies, stocks and bonds, mutual funds and unit investment trusts, variable annuities, as well as indexed annuities; but it all comes down to the investor's time horizon, and risk tolerance.

The reason why I feel very comfortable recommending annuities for a portion of the Baby Boomers' assets is because I've personally witnessed many ugly scenarios involving investing solely in equities. For every ten stories of a client quadrupling his money in equities in ten years, I've heard a hundred in which a client lost half of his account. Try explaining to Mr. Jones—who is sixty-three years old—why his account went from $550,000 to $275,000; or even worse, try explaining it to his wife. These are real-life situations that I've personally witnessed. I remember working at Morgan Stanley and hearing horror stories of some brokers in the industry who put a 100% of the client assets in equities during the boom, which led to horrendous losses. There were some days when the phone seemed to weigh 400 pounds because very few brokers were brave enough to pick up those calls and explain why that had happened. Investing 100% of your portfolio in equities requires a tolerance for losing money. I do think there's a place for equities, but such investments need to be handled in the proper way. There's a formula that's talked about in the financial industry for this: Subtract your age from one hundred, then invest that percentage of your money in equity. For example, if you're sixty years old, you should have no more than 40% of your money invested in equities. This is why you're starting to see many of the recognized banks and brokerage houses recommending annuities that are suitable to the clients; if done right, you don't have to worry about the potential of a client losing 30% of his account value in one year. This is where you hear about the power of zero. How many of the investors who lost money during those tough years wish they would've just had a return of 0%? Many would, and that's where the annuity protects the investor in the majority of cases.

$41 Trillion. The Great Wealth Transfer

Anytime the word "trillion" is used, it's something to pay attention to. The greatest wealth transfer in the history of America is taking place as we speak. The fact that 76 million Boomers are getting ready to retire has influenced many universities to do research on what that number really means. This is what Boston College said about the great wealth transfer: "Despite the economic downturn and the fall of the equity markets, the nationally noted projection that a wealth transfer of at least $41 trillion, with as high as $136 trillion, will take place in the United States by the year 2052 remains valid."

What that means is that the demand for agents and advisors to get involved in the financial industry is increasing. In order for this wealth transfer to take place, there's a need for a "middle man," and that middle man is the financial advisor. That $41 trillion will be transferred to equities, cash, or annuities, but the point is that it creates a perfect time to get involved in the business.

On my second day at Morgan Stanley (which was Tuesday, September 11th, 2001), our branch manager sat us down and told us that the next eight years were going to be some of the toughest years of our careers. He also said, however, that the greatest boom of all time in the financial industry was coming soon and that by then the industry would experience some of the greatest years it has ever had. The future year he was talking about was 2011, which was the first year that Baby Boomers started turning sixty-five years old. This is the time that many have been waiting for in the financial industry. Getting involved in the boom now will give you the opportunity to serve families while earning a great income, which in turn will allow you to spend more time with the people you love most.

CONDITION #2

CONDITION#2
OF THE PERFECT STORM:

Trust

One of the most common questions asked by entrepreneurs to-day is "What's the next boom?" So many people try to time the market, but because it is so unpredictable this rarely happens successfully. Both the tech boom and the real estate boom in the '90s were unpredictable; a few may have claimed they predicted it, but the majority missed both of the booms due to a lack of timing. If you missed the last two booms because you didn't anticipate them, it isn't your fault. If we miss getting in on the next boom, however—knowing that it's going to happen—then it *is* our fault.

In order for a sector within an industry to experience a massive boom, all of the other sectors within that industry need to stay flat for roughly ten years. Let's look at how that relates to the financial industry. Here are three simple questions to ask yourself:

1. Does America trust the banking industry today?

> "A banker is a fellow who lends you his umbrella when the sun is shining, but wants it back the minute it begins to rain."
>
> — Mark Twain

Could you or I have predicted in the early 2000s that by the end of the decade WaMu, Freddie Mac, Fannie Mae, Merrill Lynch, Lehman Brothers, Wachovia, IndyMac, Bear Stearns, New Century, and Countrywide would either be acquired, or go bankrupt? Seeing this number of banks go out of business made it very clear to many of us that it may not be a good time to put our trust in banks. Both as a career choice and as an investment option, the banking industry has lost a ton of credibility. There was once a time when investing in a CD may have sounded like a wise investment to help supplement your retirement income, but the numbers have changed. CD interest rates have had a steady decline from the high of 16% in 1981 to low of 0.28% in May of 2010. Here's what that means when it comes down to looking for a good return: If you were to invest $100,000 in a CD in 1981, by the middle of 1985 your money would've doubled to $200,000; if you were to do the same thing in May of 2010, however, your $100,000 would've doubled to $200,000 by early

2267. Yes, you read it correctly: 2267. I'm not sure about you, but I don't think that too many people have that kind of patience. This is one of many reasons why the banking industry has lost a significant portion of consumer trust.

The ten highest ninety-day CD rates in history:

Date	Return
January 1982	15.604 %
October 1981	**16.691 %**
September 1981	16.487 %
November 1981	16.424 %
August 1981	16.024 %
December 1981	15.911 %
February 1982	15.509 %
March 1982	15.491 %
April 1982	15.438 %
May 1982	15.065 %

CD interest rates showed a steady increase between the 1960s and the early 1980s. After November of 1981, the rates began to decline from the 16% interest rates that were constant that year.

The ten lowest ninety-day CD rates in history:

Date	Return	Date	Return
May 2010	**0.278 %**	October 2010	0.300 %
April 2010	0.288 %	November 2010	0.305 %
June 2010	0.288 %	May 2011	0.305 %
July 2010	0.293 %	December 2010	0.312 %
August of 2010	0.295 %	January 2011	0.319 %
September 2010	0.298 %	February 2011	0.327 %

The information provided is based on the Certificate of Deposit Index (CODI) for three-month CDs. The index is the twelve-month average of monthly average yields. The information is taken from information published monthly by the Federal Reserve.

2. Does America trust the stock market today?

There was once a time in the '90s when it was cool to be a stockbroker. Thousands of people were taking their exams to get their Series 7 license, especially after the S&P (Standard & Poor Index) posted five consecutive years with returns of 20% plus. You couldn't go a day without reading an article in the paper, or business magazines about someone who made millions trading stocks. Even Hollywood didn't want to miss this boom. Do you remember *Wall Street*, the movie starring Charlie Sheen and Michael Douglas? People across the country were constantly stealing lines from either Gordon Gekko, or Bud Fox. How about *Boiler Room*, which was where Vin Diesel first made a name for himself as a leading man? This was the era of the stockbroker.

Historical S&P 500 Index Stock Market Returns

Year	Return	Year	Return	Year	Return
1973	-14.7%	1987	5.2%	2001	-11.90%
1974	-26.5%	1988	16.8%	2002	-22.1%
1975	37.2%	1989	31.5%	2003	28.7%
1976	23.8%	1990	-3.2%	2004	10.9%
1977	-7.2%	1991	30.5%	2005	4.9%
1978	6.6%	1992	7.7%	2006	15.9%
1979	18.4%	1993	10.0%	2007	5.5%
1980	32.4%	1994	1.3%	2008	-37.0%
1981	-4.9%	1995	37.4%	2009	26.5%
1982	21.4%	1996	23.1%	2010	15.1%
1983	22.5%	1997	33.4%		
1984	6.3%	1998	28.6%		
1985	32.2%	1999	21.0%		
1986	18.5%	2000	-9.1%		

Hollywood made it cool to be a broker in the '90s, but we're living in different times. Most stockbrokers and investors no longer want to go to sleep at night, as they're too worried about how the market is going to perform in the morning. The younger generation can potentially handle the risk of losing everything and starting over; but that's not the case for the Baby Boomers, many of whom already took a big hit in 2008 and are not looking to lose another penny of their retirement account. Unless you're Bradley Cooper in *Limitless*, with access to NZT (which allows you to time the market perfectly), I suggest you look elsewhere for a career.

3. Does America trust the real estate market today?

There was a period from 2002 to 2007 when it seemed like everyone was involved in the real estate industry. Everyone wanted to call themselves an investor after making $100,000 of equity in their homes after a year. I remember clients asking me why they should purchase an annuity, or a mutual fund when they could instead buy a house with $0 down and simply sell the house a year or two later with a six-figure profit. Imagine trying to convince them that this situation wasn't going to last forever—talk about a losing battle. It was pretty ugly from 2002 to 2007 trying to build an insurance agency, as we were losing agents to the real estate industry every other day. NINA was everyone's best friend during that time. Her name stood for "No Income No Assets," which meant that someone who earned only $36,000 a year could qualify for a $750,000 loan due to the fact that the banks weren't verifying the income by requesting a W-2, or 1099. This caused a boom in the mortgage lending industry like never before. Earning a quarter of a million dollars a year during that time wasn't a surprise to many. In bigger markets in America such as California, Florida, New York, Connecticut, and a few others, brokers and loan officers were earning multiple seven-figure annual incomes. It was an era in which the streets were filled with twenty and thirty year olds in Porsches, Ferraris, Lamborghinis, Bentleys, and practically every other luxury car you can imagine.

"Greed makes the bartender buy three houses."

— Gordon Gekko

But we all know how this ended. That high level of greed from banks eventually caused a recession that almost led to a depression. At the end, we were re-reminded that the average return on real estate has always consistently been between 4 to 5%, as you can see here:

Year	Return
1890 - 2007	3.44%
1900 - 2007	4.22%
1920 - 2007	4.03%
1948 - 2007	4.87%

Or the past one hundred years:

Year	Return
1907 - 2007	3.78%

If you break it down into decade chunks we get the following:

Year	Return
1890s	0.53%
1900s	1.40%
1910s	3.30%
1920s	-0.70%
1930s	-0.45%
1940s	8.16%
1950s	2.67%
1960s	2.57%
1970s	8.12%
1980s	5.86%
1990s	2.84%
2000s	9.27%

The challenge these three industries face is that with all the attention on them, regulation is getting tighter and tighter. This means we may be going in a direction where you will no longer see mortgage companies called "Westside Mortgages," or "Johnny's Real Estate Company," seeing instead the major banks handling the majority of loans. Whenever the status quo in an industry shifts, two different groups of people always emerge: those who adapt and those who don't. There are thousands of loan officers, realtors, brokers, and bankers who were great at what they did, but they took a hit due to the economy. Many of them are now focusing on modifications, foreclosures, debt settlement, credit repair, precious metals sales, and/or short sales.

The problem with this kind of adaptation, however, is that these conditions will only exist for a few more years. When the conditions change and these strategies are no longer viable, these individuals will have to figure out another way to make money. Instead of having the luxury of thinking long term, people in the real estate industry will have to resort to another fad.

> "A fall into a ditch makes you wiser."
>
> — Chinese Proverb

Rather than seeking a quick fix, most of us are looking for an industry that we can give twenty years of our lives to, all the while knowing it will provide us with an opportunity to become financially independent and to build a personal life worth working hard for. But there's one sector left within the financial industry that is experiencing a level of growth that it hasn't had since the early '80s, and that sector is the life insurance industry. If you think about the life insurance industry, you don't hear about too many companies going out of business. As a matter of fact, I would venture to say that the average person who isn't involved in the industry couldn't name one insurance company that has gone out of business. The reason for this is that it's a stable industry that will always be around. It's not necessarily a sexy sector of the financial industry such as real estate, or banking, but it's one that allows you to earn the same kind of income (if not higher) and build your business while keeping your family life strong. Life insurance isn't a seasonal product per se like real estate, stocks, or CDs because there's always a need for life insurance. Moreover, the fact that the American people have lost trust in real estate, banking, and the stock market has created a surge of talented individuals looking into the life insurance industry as something they can devote their entire careers to. The great news is that this boom in agents getting involved in the life insurance industry is just beginning. Now is a great time to launch a career in this industry, which provides the opportunity of serving the consumer while also building your own agency. This boom will go on for the next ten years (from 2012 to 2022). It won't last forever, and so the key to success is launching your career as soon as possible.

You may still be asking why you should choose a career in the life insurance business, but let me explain further why recruiting will be at an all-time high in the next decade. *The Wall Street Journal* did an article on March 19th, 2010, titled "A Hot Job for Hard Times: The Life Insurance Agent." The article explained that the life insurance industry has been declining since 1974; but despite this, the article went on to say, the industry is about to experience a level of growth like never before. According to the article, "The number of U.S. life insurance agents affiliated with a specific company today is down nearly a third since the 1970s, to 174,000, according to LIMRA." We're talking about going from over half a million licensed life insurance agents to only 174,000; I would say that's a significant decline.

The first thing that comes to mind is "why?" Well, prior to the '80s, being a life insurance agent was a common profession, but due to some of the following events, the number of licensed agents in the industry started declining. For decades the big life insurance companies built their agencies by focusing on getting their new recruits to pass their life insurance license requirements as soon as possible, but then a few distractions showed up. In 1970, there were approximately 360 mutual funds, with $48 billion in combined assets. At the end of 2010, there were over 15,000 mutual funds of all types in the United States, with combined assets of $13.1 trillion. I'm not sure about you, but I would consider that a boom. Additionally, the introduction of money market funds in the high-interest rate environment of the late 1970s boosted industry growth dramatically. The first retail index fund, First Index Investment Trust, was formed in 1976 by The Vanguard Group (which was led by John Bogle, who in 2004 was recognized by *Time Magazine* as one of the world's one hundred most powerful and influential people). It was the fad to be involved in the sale of mutual funds or money market accounts. Some money markets were offering returns in the high 10% range during that time, which was very attractive to Baby Boomers. Today, that same money market fund barely gives you a return of 0.1%—that's not 1%, but *0.1%*. Money markets are no longer used as an investment as much as they're used for emergency funds.

Baby Boomers at that time were concerned with accumulating wealth, and mutual funds sure sounded like a good investment.

That caused many insurance companies to shift their focus. They had new agents get their mutual fund license (Series 6 & 63) instead of their life insurance license. Then came the '90s, during which time the tech boom showed up out of nowhere. In response, investors wanted to buy individual stocks instead of mutual funds. The license needed to sell individual stocks is the Series 7, which meant that the insurance companies had to once again change their priorities. Instead of having new agents get their insurance license, or their mutual fund license, they now needed them to get their Series 7 license. That lasted for a decade, until the real estate boom started in the early 2000s. With the introduction of new programs called "Negative Amortization," "Pick a Payment," or many other names, it became very easy for families to qualify for loans with payments they could afford to make for the time being. That boom inspired several insurance companies to get their agents to start putting focus on the real estate industry. Whether they encouraged agents to get their real estate license, or to learn how to sell HELOCs (home equity line of credit), companies once again changed the priorities of licensing for new recruits.

As a result of this constant re-prioritization, it's no wonder that the industry went from having over 500,000 licensed agents in the 1970s to 174,000 in 2010. But here's the good news: We are right back at square one, returning to the industry that America trusted for decades. That industry is life insurance.

> "The best time to plant a tree is twenty years ago. The second best time is now."
>
> — Chinese Proverb

This is just the beginning. The next ten to twenty years are going to be some of the greatest recruiting years of the life insurance industry. I remember the news in 2006 showing thousands of people going to the Los Angeles Convention Center to take their real estate exams, people who had no idea that there was only one year left in that boom. When you see thousands of people getting on board, you know the boom has already passed you by. For the first time in history, the California Department of Insurance has lowered the qualification for passing the life insurance licensing exam to 60% instead of the traditional 70%. Imagine what it's going to look like when the current number of 174,000 licensed agents gets back up to 500,000, or even a million over the next twenty years. It would be a good idea to consider building an agency during this boom within the insurance industry before the field gets too crowded and the opportunity diminishes with time.

> "If you want one year of prosperity, grow grain. If you want ten years of prosperity, grow trees. If you want one hundred years of prosperity, grow people."
>
> — Chinese Proverb

CONDITION #3

CONDITION #3
OF THE PERFECT STORM:

-Average Age of Fifty-Six Years Old-

According to LIMRA and *The Wall Street Journal*, the average age of a life insurance agent is fifty-six years old. The reason why this is so important is that the majority of the experienced agents at that age are no longer selling, or training new recruits. They've earned the right to live the lifestyle they've worked so hard to earn. These are the individuals you normally see golfing on a daily basis. I'm not judging them for having paid the price of twenty years or more of dedicated service and now wanting to spend their time with their grandchildren, but the industry is never the less going to take a hit because of their choice. The average age of life insurance agents has gone up every single year for the last two decades, meaning that the industry isn't attracting a lot of new blood. You don't hear too many students at USC, NYU, or Duke say that they want to sell life insurance when they finish school.

But why is that? If you read the book *The Millennial Movement*, you'll realize what the younger generation is after. They're not necessarily looking to make money to drive Ferraris and live in big houses. Just look at how long it took Mark Zuckerberg to buy a home. You don't see him driving a Ferrari, or wearing a Rolex watch. Although there's nothing wrong with expensive cars or watches, the important thing to Zuckerberg is making history. Money is not the central goal of the Millennial Generation. Instead their goal is to make a difference and do something that's never been done before. Too many insurance companies are not speaking the Millennial Generation's language, and because of that the industry doesn't seem attractive enough for them to get involved in. For the longest time, the life insurance industry has had the reputation of being boring. However, the good news is that Millennials are starting to understand how much need there is in the industry, and as a result they're looking for the right opportunity to run with. If you're a Millennial and you want to be part of the solution, your country is waiting for you to get involved in the life insurance industry and be part of the movement of protecting as many families as possible.

Jorge Pelayo is a perfect example of someone who wanted to be the hero of his family. He knew that immediately after high school he was expected to take care of his loved ones. His parents did their best to raise their three children with the highest level of respect and values, and at a young age Jorge started dabbling in different business ventures in order to help support his family. At the age of nineteen he was introduced to the life insurance industry while going to school. He decided to get his license on the side and give the industry a shot as a part-timer. Very quickly, he started noticing the potential the business offered, and so he went full time to build his own agency. He's now in his mid-twenties running an agency of close to two hundred licensed agents, an agency that is growing very rapidly. He's earning the kind of an income that most executives don't earn after working at a firm for twenty, or more years. At the same time, he has become an example to others his age that they too can build a respectable business and earn an incredible living if they take themselves and their business seriously. Jorge has been able to travel all over the world as well. One of his dreams was to take his entire family to Hawaii. Just last year, he took eight of his family members on an all-expense paid trip to Hawaii for a week. Another one of his dreams was to one day visit his family in Puerto Rico, which he had never had a chance to do. He ended up going to visit Puerto Rico, as well as five different islands in the Caribbean with his younger brother, who now looks at him as his role model. His younger brother already talks about what he wants to do when he turns eighteen years old: become a life insurance agent. During this journey, Jorge has developed a strong faith in God. As part of this faith, he sees the insurance business as a vehicle to allow him to empower others and serve his generation with the highest standards possible.

The Millennial Generation is much different than the Baby Boomers. They want the people at the top of the company to be part of their generation so they can understand and relate to them. This isn't to say that they don't respect their elders. But just like in sports, this generation wants to watch the upcoming heroes instead of the established greats. We know Michael Jordan is recognized as the greatest basketball player of all time, but no one wants to watch him play today. Everyone wants to watch the next twenty-five year old who is the future of the NBA. Similarly, today's youth is looking to run with players like LeBron James, Kevin Durant, or Derrick Rose.

That same principle is very much present in the life insurance business. Millennials are looking for companies that are run by young CEOs and presidents who understand today's world. We're living in an era in which the fastest growing companies are being led by CEOs in their twenties and thirties. I'm not just talking about the field leaders, or the VPs, but rather the president and CEO running the company. Zuckerberg is in his late twenties, Google's CEO and president are both in their thirties, and Zappos' CEO Tony Hsieh is also in his thirties. However, in the financial industry, the leaders running the company are on average in their late fifties to sixties. Even Boomers nowadays are seeing the Millennials' viewpoint. They also want younger leaders who are constantly innovating and staying on top of trends. I've repeatedly said that we are only decades away from having a President of the United States of America who will be in his late thirties, and these young business leaders are proof that we are moving in that direction.

Things are changing faster than ever before, especially regarding marketing. Commercials on TV are no longer as effective as they were twenty, or thirty years ago, but platforms such as Twitter, Facebook, YouTube, and blogs are incredibly successful, and are accepted communication tools. For example, there's a video on YouTube called "Charlie Bit My Finger," which has gotten 448,177,606 hits in less than five years. Yet the most recent Super Bowl drew only 111 million viewers, and that's the *Super Bowl* we're talking about. According to ESPN, companies paid $3.5 million for a thirty second commercial for Super Bowl 2012. With that in mind, I would love to see how much it would cost to have "Charlie Bit My Finger" stay on national television long enough to rack up over 448 million views! Clearly, marketing has become cheaper, faster, and more effective than ever before, and Millennials are master marketers.

The evolution of digital marketing is an unstoppable reality. People no longer care if you have a website so much as if you have a LinkedIn, Facebook, or a Twitter account. As a broker in the industry, digital technology gives you the opportunity to recruit and develop agents that are the future of this industry. You get the opportunity to set an example for them and develop them into leaders, something America is desperately in need of. This becomes a perfect formula for the two generations to work together. When Boomers and Millennials realize they both need each other, they could potentially form a winning team.

Millennials need Boomers for the following reasons:

1. Sharing life experiences.
2. Learning the right values and principles.
3. Having someone who can teach them about what it is to be a man, or a woman, as we have way too many adults in America who are still boys and girls.
4. Learning from the Baby Boomer's mistakes.
5. Having a mentor.

Boomers need Millennials for the following reasons:

1. Keeping them young and active.
2. Feeling a sense of fulfillment for developing leaders.
3. Learning the current trends on social media and communication.
4. Learning some modern dance moves, which probably wouldn't be a bad idea!

The fact of the matter is that both Millennials and Boomers are going to take advantage of the boom. If they can learn to work as a team and tap into each other's strengths, they will be all the more successful in their endeavors.

The story of Jason and Diana Graziani comes to mind, both graduates of USC who completed college with the desire to do something special with their lives. Jason was raised by a single mother, who raised three boys by herself. At a very young age, Jason's mother became disabled, but she didn't let that keep her from raising strong boys. Every one of her boys earned their four-year degrees from respectable universities, where they each paid the tuition by themselves. Jason was looking for an industry he could get involved in to make a big impact in other people's lives. After a short stint in the corporate world, he and Diana ended up getting involved in the life insurance industry. They started part time while working at their full-time jobs. Very shortly, Jason went full-time with life insurance to build his business. Just like in any business, the first two years were difficult, but with support he was able to become a broker fairly quickly. By his third year in the business, he was already earning over a six-figure annual income, which quickly became a multi-six-figure income by his fifth year in business. He accomplished all of this while in his mid to late twenties. As a result of his success and dedication, he was able to retire his mom and get her a place right next to where he and his wife live. They also have been fortunate to be able to travel all over the world, visiting Hawaii, St. Maarten, Puerto Rico, Barbados, Pebble Beach, St. Lucia, Antigua, Cancun, Banff Canada, and many other locations. He has major plans of eventually getting involved in politics to make a significant impact on America. One of his goals in life is to be a great example to the Millennial Generation, with the mission of turning boys to men (and he's not referring to the R&B band).

LEMONADE

CONDITION #4

CONDITION #4
OF THE PERFECT STORM:

—— The Era of the Entrepreneur ——

According to the Bureau of Labor statistics, the following states experienced their highest unemployment rate in the history during the unemployment crises of 2009 to 2011:

State or District	Unemployment rate (seasonally adjusted)
California	12.4%
Colorado	9.0%
Connecticut	9.4%
Florida	11.4%
Georgia	10.5%
Kansas	7.6%
Nevada	12.0%
North Carolina	11.4%
Rhode Island	11.9%
South Carolina	12.0%

Current Unemployment Rate April 2012

State or District	Unemployment Rate (seasonally adjusted)
Nevada	12.3%
Rhode Island	11.0%
California	10.9%
District of Columbia	9.9%
North Carolina	9.9%
Mississippi	9.5%
Florida	9.4%
Georgia	9.1%
Illinois	9.1%
South Carolina	9.1%
New Jersey	9.0%
Michigan	8.8%
Oregon	8.8%
Arizona	8.7%
Kentucky	8.7%
New York	8.5%
Indiana	8.4%
United States (mean)[5]	8.2%

United States Unemployment Rate

Year	Rate	Year	Rate	Year	Rate
1950	5.3%	1980	7.1%	1998	4.5%
1952	3.0%	1982	9.7%	1999	4.2%
1954	5.5%	1984	7.5%	2000	4.0%
1956	4.1%	1986	7.0%	2001	4.7%
1958	6.8%	1987	6.2%	2002	5.8%
1960	5.5%	1988	5.5%	2003	6.0%
1962	5.5%	1989	5.3%	2004	5.5%
1964	5.2%	1990	5.6%	2005	5.1%
1966	3.8%	1991	6.8%	2006	4.6%
1968	3.6%	1992	7.5%	2007	4.6%
1970	4.9%	1993	6.9%	2008	5.8%
1972	5.6%	1994	6.1%	2009	9.3%
1974	5.6%	1995	5.6%	2010	9.6%
1976	7.7%	1996	5.4%	2011	8.9%
1978	6.1%	1997	4.9%		

As a nation, we have not experienced three consecutive years of 8.9% or higher in unemployment rate since the Great Depression. To put things more into perspective, we haven't had a year above 7% unemployment in the last twenty years. The average has been somewhere between 4 and 6% since 1992.

> "My son is now an 'entrepreneur.' That's what you're called when you don't have a job."
>
> — Ted Turner

Historically speaking, every time we've experienced a rise in unemployment, we have also seen a tremendous surge in entrepreneurship. With record breaking years in unemployment, more Americans are starting to realize that the only way to have freedom is to become an entrepreneur.

> "Job security is gone. The driving force of a career must come from the individual."
>
> — Earl Nightingale

Sometimes having our backs against the wall reminds us what we're really capable of. It shows us that we still have a fight in us. For those who were high school, or college athletes, it brings out a side of you that we haven't seen since hell week in football, or in any other sport where you had to fight to get playing time. We are so much more capable than we think we are.

I would've never imagined being where I'm currently at in life financially. My family and I escaped a war-stricken Iran to go to Germany when I was a child, where we stayed at a refugee camp for two years with the dreams of finally making it to the land of all opportunities. All immigrants who fight to come to America do so for two reasons: control and freedom in their own lives, something we all aspire to have. We want the control to raise our kids in a community that we feel comfortable in, to put them in schools that provide the best possible education, as well as a good athletic program. We want the control to take our families on nice vacations every year to enjoy those magical moments that we will forever remember. We want the freedom to practice any religion without fear, the freedom to earn as much money as we'd like without being called greedy, or selfish, and the freedom to have access to a cell phone, internet, newspaper, or TV show that we desire to watch. In America, we have those freedoms, and we even have the freedom to have our own opinions with which others in turn have the freedom to disagree with. But although we have certain inalienable rights simply by virtue of being citizens of this country, many of the controls and freedoms we desire come at the price of being an entrepreneur.

We're facing some challenging times in America today. We often hear different opinions on how to fix our financial problems, but the key is to go back and find out how we made this country great in the first place. Cleon Skousen, author of *The 5000 Year Leap*, writes about the twenty-eight principles of liberty that our founding fathers came up with. Principle 15 tells us this: "The highest level of prosperity occurs when there is a free-market economy and a minimum of government regulations."

This means that our nation's prosperity depends upon a climate of wholesome stimulation with four basic freedoms in operation:

1. The freedom to **TRY.**
2. The freedom to **BUY.**
3. The freedom to **SELL.**
4. The freedom to **FAIL.**

It's important for us to encourage and challenge one another to go back to what built this country, which was the everyday entrepreneur. We need more people to try and fail in order to have the opportunity to buy and sell. Our government is afraid of having people fail, yet they want to encourage everyone to keep buying things to grow the economy. I'm a big believer of free enterprise because that's the only true way of having freedom. And one of the most tried and true ways of earning the freedom that America offers is to be an entrepreneur. You'll get paid exactly what you're worth; if you earned a million a year, you earned it, and if you earn only $30,000 a year, you also earned that. That's the great thing about the free market: It will pay us based on our efforts and on the competence of the business we're involved in. Your earning potential has nothing to do with your last name, the inheritance you received, how high you can jump, or how tall you are. Instead it's all reliant on what you put into your work.

I recently interviewed David Walker, the former Comptroller General of the United States of America, and he specifically said that one of the main drivers for restoring America will be the day-to-day entrepreneur. It's time for the entrepreneurs of America to get together as leaders and fight to bring back the free enterprise system, thereby restoring hope to American families. Entrepreneurs don't do what they do just to become wealthy. They do it to give back to their local communities. Some of the greatest hospitals, churches, and schools of higher learning exist because an entrepreneur decided to use his resources to start a charity. The perfect timing in the insurance business creates the condition for the next generation of entrepreneurs to rise up and make history. This is a cause worth fighting for.

So often we're told to follow the system to the tee and it will produce success. Len and Tasha Cooper did exactly that. Len Cooper was raised by a single mother in Inglewood, California, which was at that time a gang-infested environment. He grew up being constantly told to go get a degree in order to live the American Dream and have freedom over his own destiny. Taking that advice to a whole different level, he ended up getting his bachelor's degree, as well as two master's degrees and a PhD from Claremont University in Education. He ended up being the youngest principal in all of San Bernardino County. His wife Tasha also took schooling very seriously and got her master's degree, which led her to being a school psychologist. Doing their best to raise their two boys, they finally came to a conclusion that there was a ceiling to the amount of income they could earn if they kept going in the direction they were going. After much consideration, Len decided to become an entrepreneur. He looked at many different businesses until he decided to get involved in the life insurance and the financial industries. He and his wife now run a very successful agency that continues to expand all across Southern California, as well as Arizona. The industry has given them the opportunity to travel all over the world while taking their twelve and fourteen-year-old sons with them. Len hasn't even been in the industry all that long, less than five years. He is now looking at this industry as a vehicle to allow him to really make a major, positive impact in the world of education.

I haven't met one person yet who wouldn't mind being financially independent, yet some of our choices are not congruent with our desires. For instance, think about the wealthiest person who you know. I'm not talking about Warren Buffett, or Bill Gates, but someone who you know either in your immediate family, or as an acquaintance. Now here's the kicker that tells us what we need to do in order to have the opportunity of becoming wealthy: Is the person you're thinking about an employee of a company, or an entrepreneur? Chances are, your answer was an entrepreneur. If that's the case, what makes you think that you can be wealthy by simply having a job?

Jack Gibbs went to Alaska in 1969 from the East Coast for vacation and never left. He worked at Sears, but he was recruited by an insurance company while in his mid-twenties. He started doing life insurance part time and quit his job at Sears. He was the number one personal producer for thirteen years in Alaska at Academy Life, which only served the military 100% of the time. The industry allowed Jack to spend the summers with his kids as well as travel with his son Bo when he got involved in competitive tennis. By the time Bo turned thirteen, he was flying all across the country playing tennis in professional tournaments.

The fact that Jack Gibbs was involved in the life insurance business allowed his younger son to pursue his dreams of becoming a professional tennis player. Right after college, Bo played in tournaments all across Europe, including Switzerland, France, Germany, Italy, Spain, Austria, and the Netherlands. Bo said that the biggest lesson he took away from his experience abroad was that he came back to the United States with the conviction that he lived in the greatest country in the world. "It was obviously great to be able to take tennis as far as I could go and be able to close that chapter in my life not having to look back with any feeling of what if," Bo went on. "This would not have been remotely possible if my dad wasn't involved in an industry where he could earn the kind of income and have the kind of flexibility that allowed him to help us pursue our dreams during our youth. My brother, sister, and I were all awarded athletic scholarships because we had the freedom to not worry about anything but sports and school."

Inspired by their father's example, both of Jack's sons followed in his footsteps and got involved in the life insurance business.

Jack trained his older son Trey, who in turn trained Bo, the younger son. In 1998, during his first year in business. During that time, Bo had a long distance relationship with Alison, the love of his life, whom he met at Indiana University. With the flexibility of the life insurance field, he and Alison decided to move to Chicago to experience living in a big city. In 1999, they were married at a chapel at Indiana University, where they initially met. They eventually moved to Atlanta, where they are currently raising three children (including a set of twins) and living their dreams. They live in an exclusive community in a house right under 10,000 square feet, and the industry has given them the opportunity to see the world together. Being a big sports fan, Bo has had the opportunity to go to the Final Four, Cowboys playoff games, the MLB World Series, hockey playoffs, the Kentucky Derby, the Preakness, the French Open in Paris twice, the U.S. Open five times, the Augusta National Tournament twice (which he also played in twice), and ten NASCAR races, all the while traveling across the country in private jets.

Jack Gibbs and his sons are a prime example of what the life insurance business offers to those who not only want to make a great living but also have a great life. They are leaving a family legacy of success, one that they can pass down proudly to their children and grandchildren.

CONDITION #5

CONDITION #5
OF THE PERFECT STORM:

—— The Need For Life Insurance ——

There was a period in 2002 and 2003 when my friends and I used to go to the El Torito restaurant near our office at least three times a week. The manager working there was named Jacob. Jacob had a wife and three kids. At the time, he was thirty-nine years old and perfectly healthy. You couldn't assume by looking at him that he had any health issues. His wife was raising the kids at home while he was working. The challenge with his wife was that she didn't speak any English, which meant that Jacob was earning the only income they were depending on. One day one of my agents talked to him about the importance of life insurance. They set up a time to get together at Jacob's house to possibly put a life insurance policy together for him. But at the end of their appointment, Jacob didn't see a need to purchase a policy because he was young and thought it was a waste of money. The agent reaffirmed the importance of having a policy, especially with the situation that he was in with his wife and three children, but still, Jacob didn't see any value in moving forward with a policy, whether it was a term, or a permanent one. The agent left disappointed with himself that he couldn't serve the family despite his best effort.

A week went by before we went back to the restaurant, and while there we asked our waiter about Jacob. The waiter had the most disturbing look on his face when asked the question and told us that Jacob had a heart attack the night before in his sleep and never woke up. He died at the age of thirty-nine, leaving behind very little savings and no life insurance policy for his wife and three kids. I'll never forget how my stomach felt when I first heard the news. There was a sense of failure as well as concern for the family, and the feeling that we could've tried a bit harder to convince them of the importance of life insurance. However, we all knew that the agent did all that he could do. But from that moment on, I adopted a totally different perspective on what it meant to be a life insurance agent. I was reminded of just how important and honorable it was to serve and protect as many families as possible. It no longer was just a job or a career. Ever since that day, I wake up every morning knowing that there is a bigger purpose to my career than just a paycheck.

The non-profit organization Life Insurance Foundation for Education (LIFE) has done an excellent job of educating as well as creating awareness for life insurance needs. One of the most recent interviews they did was with Lamar Odom, the former Los Angeles Laker who was the national spokesperson for Life Insurance Awareness Month in 2011. In the interview he shares a story of how life insurance was one of the main reasons why he was able to make it to the NBA. His quest to the NBA began in a single-parent household in Queens, N.Y. His mother Cathy earned a decent income working as a corrections officer, and with that income she sent him to a Catholic school because of concerns about the public schools in their rough neighborhood. Unfortunately, she didn't live to see Lamar succeed as an athlete. Cathy died of colon cancer when he was only twelve years old.

Lamar's mother never expected to die at such a young age, but thankfully she did not leave her son's future to chance. Because she had life insurance, Lamar was able to continue his private school education. When he graduated high school at eighteen, life insurance again impacted his life when he was already considered one of the best young basketball players in the country. Because he was financially stable as a result of his mothers life insurance proceeds, he had the chance to attend college for several years. "Too many Americans haven't done the kind of planning that my mom did," says Lamar. "They don't have life insurance because they don't think they'll ever need it. I'm sure my mom didn't think that she'd die at thirty-five, but that didn't stop her from doing the responsible thing."

Think about how many childhood athletes with a chance to go to the next level, weren't able to do so due to a death in the family that caused them to start working early and sacrifice their dreams. How many young people with aspirations of being doctors one day who, because of the loss of the bread winner without a life insurance policy, are forced to drop out of college and get jobs to support their family? This is one of the many reasons why a life insurance agent's work is honorable. You may not get the glory at the sale, or even in the near future, but when the day comes that the life insurance policy needs to be put to use, you will forever be remembered by the ever so grateful family members.

The Basics of Life Insurance

Life insurance is probably one of the simplest products to learn about. You have two choices when buying life insurance: You can either buy a term, or a permanent policy. The easiest way to explain the two is to look at term as renting a house and permanent as owning one. If you can't afford to buy a house, you rent one. The advantage of renting a house is the fact that you can move at any time and it's cheaper than buying. But the disadvantage is that renting doesn't build any equity. The same goes for a term policy: A term policy is cheap, but it doesn't build equity. On the other hand, a permanent policy is like owning a house. The mortgage payment may be a bit higher than renting, however, over the long haul, you end up building equity. That's how a permanent policy works. You pay a bit higher than a term policy, but it builds equity and lasts until the ages of 100 to 120.

Both term and permanent policies have a place where they're effective. Many people will argue with each other and tell you that the only way to go is to buy term and invest the difference, while other agents will say buying permanent policies is the way to go. I'm here to tell you that one size doesn't fit everyone. I would encourage you to find out for yourself which one makes the most sense for you. This is another reason why I'm an advocate of encouraging people to get involved in the financial industry to learn for themselves the secrets of money.

When you look at some of the statistics today, you realize how much of a need there is for more life insurance agents out there. The Life Insurance and Market Research Association (LIMRA) released its research findings in September of 2011, showcasing a few facts about life insurance. Some of the numbers on this report were staggering:

- The proportion of U.S. adults with life insurance protection has declined to an all-time low of 41%, which means that a total of 95 million U.S. adults have no life insurance at all.
- Only one in ten insured adults own both permanent and term life insurance—half as many as in 2004.
- Young males (ages eighteen to twenty-four) are less likely than in past decades to be starting their adult years with any individual life insurance. Only 13% had individual life policies in 2010, compared with 30% in 1998.

Although these are simply statistics that you're looking at, I want you to think about how life insurance affects the economy.

Think about how many families would be relying on the government after a loss if the bread winner hadn't taken the time to purchase a life insurance policy. The surviving spouse would have to replace the income somehow, and normally that happens through government assistance—money which, by the way, is generated by collecting taxes. That means you and I are paying for someone who either didn't see value in purchasing a life insurance policy, or didn't have the opportunity of an agent presenting them with different options of life insurance.

What's most amazing in today's society is that we've been conditioned to think that there's more value in insuring our cell phones, cars, jewelry, art work, home, and many other things, yet it's not a big deal to put off insuring our own lives—something that our family is counting on far more than a cell phone. Think about how much safer you and I feel driving on the streets ever since auto insurance became mandatory. Have you ever gotten in a car accident where the other driver was at fault yet wasn't insured? Who had to pay for the damage? How did you feel about it? What happened to the cost of your auto insurance policy? And though auto insurance is necessary, which is more important when it comes down to it: your car or your life?

Some will say that life insurance is expensive, but the truth of the matter is that life insurance has never been cheaper than it is today. This is because life insurance is all about life expectancy, and we're living much longer today than we ever have before. This in turn means almost anyone can afford life insurance. What's needed are agents who can create that awareness for families and help them see the consequences of what can happen if they're not protected. Basic math tells us if more families are protected, there will be less chances of another tax consequence for the hard-working American families who are doing their part. Life insurance creates an independent atmosphere rather than a dependent one.

All of these statistics are happening during a time when the total number of life insurance agents has decreased from 500,000 to 174,000. A break down like this in which the need for life insurance is increasing while the number of agents is decreasing creates an explosive opportunity in the industry. This isn't a myth. All of the numbers in this book reflect factual events that are taking place right now. Nothing is hypothetical. This is the reality. Economics 101 teaches supply and demand, and there is a major demand for life insurance agents to help protect as many families as possible, but we currently have a very limited supply of life insurance agents. The life insurance industry is experiencing the beginning stages of a boom as the demand is answered. This boom is causing many agents to relocate to new, growing markets. Chad Terpstra, for example, grew up fifty miles south of Des Moines in New Sharon, Iowa, a town with a population of 1,200. He moved to California with the dream of being the next big Hollywood star. While in Los Angeles, he was introduced to the life insurance and financial industries in 2004. By 2009, he started seeing the opportunity for building an agency instead of just being a producer selling policies. With the flexibility the industry offers, he decided to relocate to Fort Lauderdale, Florida, to build his agency. He and his business partners Jonathan Mason and Kehinde Thomas now run a respectable operation that continues to expand all across the East Coast. You're starting to hear more stories of people moving to new territories because of the opportunity that exists for expansion. There's a tremendous amount of demand for agents all across the country.

The life insurance business is attracting people from all walks of life. Initially I thought the most successful people in the industry would be those with prior experience in sales, but my assumption couldn't have been further from the truth. I've had the honor of working with thousands of agents over the last ten years in the financial services industry, primarily in the life insurance business, many with no prior sales experience. The majority of the agents whom I've seen do extremely well came from a career that attracted individuals who enjoyed serving and helping people. It becomes a very natural fit for them to transition from what they're doing into life insurance.

Honorable Professions

An honorable profession is something worth investing your life in. There's honor in any job that someone does well and with enthusiasm, but there are some professions that simply deserve our honor and respect. As human beings we all seek to be part of something bigger than ourselves. Hollywood has made billions of dollars by creating fictional characters such as the Hulk, Superman, Spiderman, and many others to connect with audiences who value the fantasy of the good guy saving the world. Enjoyable as these characters are, it is important that we emphasize who the real superheroes of America really are. Heroic professions are ones that individuals choose because of their desire to serve and protect others. Some of the professions on the following list may be ones that you don't think of as particularly honorable, until the day that person is helping you. Some of these careers simply don't get the credit they deserve despite the fact that they are full of real-life heroes. They may not be the highest paid or the most recognized, but the world wouldn't be the same without them.

1. Military Personnel

One of the many things that I liked about being in the U.S. Army was waking up every morning with the knowledge that what I did was honorable. It was a certain feeling that words can't describe; something you have to experience to fully understand.

The sense of pride that came from just walking through the mall or the local community in my uniform was priceless. There was great worth in knowing that the greatest nation on earth was counting on me to protect it. Civilians might not think about military personnel on a daily basis as they go to work, but when a crisis like 9/11 takes place, they're glad the men and women of the armed forces are there to put their lives on the line if need be. In many cases, soldiers spend months, if not years, away from their loved ones. While some may complain about missing a favorite TV show, or the big game due to our jobs, or commitments, there are soldiers missing the birth of their newborn, or the moment their toddler takes the first steps. These are just some of the sacrifices our armed forces make for a larger cause. Some make the ultimate sacrifice for a cause greater than their own lives—the cause of liberty, humanity, or the defeat of evil.

When I first arrived at the 101st Airborne Division in September of 1997, we got word that a movie was coming out that featured our unit. The entire base went on a rotation of watching this movie in a theater on base that could fit around 800 soldiers. The

movie was *Saving Private Ryan.* Just imagine how electrified the theater was at the end when Captain John Miller (played by Tom Hanks) spoke his dying words to Private James Francis Ryan (played by Matt Damon): "Earn this—earn it." Every single one of us in that theater had eyes filled with tears of

honor and hearts filled with the desire to earn it. Whether you've been in the military, or not, that was a powerful moment because ultimately we all want to earn it. There's not one person in the world who doesn't want to make a positive impact. We all want to leave a legacy behind in which our grandchildren remember the impact we made.

Former military personnel do extremely well in life insurance because of their natural instinct to protect individuals. Their work ethic also serves them well in business.

2. Teachers

Most of us know that teachers are not the highest paid professionals out there, but the job is rewarding in other ways. If you think about some of the people who influenced you the most in life, odds are you would remember a teacher or two. It could've been twenty years ago, but you probably still remember the teacher who inspired you, believed in you, or challenged you.

At Glendale High School, I had a teacher named Ms. Sinclair who made a big impact on my life. She was a little shy of five feet tall and weighed maybe 110 pounds, but she walked around as if she were ten feet tall. She commanded the entire class with her words. She believed in her students and encouraged us, but she also pushed us to be better and to reach higher. She was a Major in the Army Reserve and a big part of the reason that I eventually joined the Army. Later in life, when I was invited back to high school as a keynote speaker, I spent the first fifteen minutes of my hour telling the students about Ms. Sinclair and the enormous influence she had on me. I still see her as an angel that God put in my life.

The life insurance business is simply about teaching basic financial concepts to individual families, which makes it a very simple, successful fit for teachers. Many teachers sell life insurance as a part-time career to supplement their full-time income during the three months they get off each year.

3. Police Officers

When we see a cop in our rear view mirror, we typically don't get a warm, fuzzy feeling of appreciation for this profession. In fact, we can get pretty argumentative and rude toward the police—that is until someone breaks into your home, or office, and they are there at 5:00 am to make sure everyone is okay. How often do we hear stories about a police officer getting shot, or injured on the job? That's someone's husband, daughter, or brother who just took a bullet for the community. Most police officers have a strong desire to see justice and protect the innocent. Sure, you can find the occasional example of a cop who abuses his, or her powers, but let's focus on the thousands who do their job with honor and a desire "to serve and protect."

It is very common for police officers to have a career outside of the full-time job of law enforcement. They're either involved in security work or sales. Life insurance is an excellent fit for them, especially since their motto is about protecting and serving.

4. Firefighters

Unlike police officers, firefighters actually get quite a bit of respect and recognition for what they do. September 11th was a vivid reminder for all of us that firefighters run toward danger when any sane person would run away. I live in Southern California, and the wildfires here can get pretty ferocious. Thousands here know that they owe their homes, possessions, and sometimes their very lives to the brave men and women who stand between the flames and their world. Firefighters don't do it for the money, or glory, they do it because they are driven to save the lives and livelihoods of others.

Firefighters are successful in the life insurance business for many of the same reasons police officers are.

5. Nurses

Other than the birth of a new baby, we rarely go to the hospital for a happy reason. I'd never been much of a fan of hospitals, until my father had a major heart attack that caused him to stay in the hospital for a month at the UCLA medical center. That experience influenced me to have a different level of appreciation for what nurses do. They're living angels to many families and patients who count on them while they recover. Nurses see people at their most difficult, painful, and stressful moments. Sick and hurting people look to their nurse to comfort them, listen to them, and take care of them. Nurses work long and demanding hours, sometimes dealing with tragedy and unavoidable death.

Their reward is found in the moments in which they see a patient get well and go home, in no small part because of their tireless and dedicated efforts. We may not always like a nurse poking us with a needle, but many of us will have days in our lives when a nurse will be the one getting us to healthier times.

Nurses have a gift of patience when it comes to dealing with people, which helps with showing families the different options they have in getting their finances in order. The compassion and dedication of nurses helps them to succeed in the industry.

6. Parents

It's a difficult task today to be a parent. There are more things to guard your kids from than there were twenty years ago. The internet has become an amazing educational tool, as well as a dangerous playground for children. Moreover, we live in a culture today where kids are not taught to respect their parents, and parents are in turn afraid to discipline their children. But many parents aren't afraid to give the love, guidance, and discipline children and teenagers need. Moms and dads are responsible for raising the next generation of leaders and thinkers. Being a parent is perhaps the most under appreciated job because it is often not even recognized as a job. As a society, we need to keep the standard of parenting high, and that starts by recognizing that being a parent is the most important job we will ever do. For every bad parent, there are hundreds that are day-to-day heroes. Tell them what a great job they are doing, whether they are your own parents, or parents you know in your community.

It's very easy for a parent to sit with other parents and show them the importance of life insurance and the role it plays in the future of their loved ones.

7. Doctors

With the current controversial health care debate, many doctors have been criticized for making too much money, or charging too much for services. But if you're willing to be in school for twenty years and spend hundreds of thousands of dollars for an education, you have earned the right to get compensated for it. Even though medicine is a well compensated profession, most doctors do not get into it for the money. Most doctors I have met wanted to be doctors since they were little. They have a powerful drive to help people, save lives, and make a difference. When a tenacious doctor works to save your loved one, you realize that is what he, or she does every day for so many families.

Most full-time doctors whom I've seen get involved in the financial services industry did so originally out of a desire to get their own finances in order. Getting involved in the industry allows them to learn as much as they can about how money works. Some of them end up making a career out of it.

8. Clergy

Talk about a full-time job—when you're the head of a church, you work 24/7. Pastors and priests never truly have time off because they are always responsible for their congregation. The pastor must console and pray for the wife whose husband just left her and their three children, or for the church member who just lost his home and has nowhere to live. When the church is short on funds for charitable work, it is the pastor who must deliver the unpopular message to the congregation on the importance of tithing. Perhaps most importantly, a clergyman, or woman is the face of God's love to so many people.

It's true that there have been clergy who did not live up to that responsibility, and unfortunately one bad example can overshadow the good work of thousands of other pastors serving God and their communities with honor and grace. But don't judge a church based on a prior bad experience. I was once very critical of churches and not at all open to the idea of anything to do with religion. It was only after several collisions with rock bottom that I realized I couldn't rise above life's challenges by myself and started seeking the truth. Whether you belong to a small congregation, or a large one, let your clergy know how much you appreciate them. Believe it or not, you could be the first person to do so.

More and more churches are starting to see the importance of not shying away from teaching their congregation about how money works. Many of them are starting to set up workshops and encourage families to attend and learn the basics of money. Becoming a life insurance agent on the side is a natural fit for members of the clergy.

9. Engineers

Whether you're driving across the river on a bridge, using any kind of electronic equipment, downloading software to your computer, or flying to another continent, you owe thanks to groups of engineers who spend countless hours developing and advancing many technologies. Engineers have made things easier, faster, cleaner, simpler, and cheaper for us to use. Chances are you're reading this book on a Kindle, Nook, or an iPad, which was designed by an engineer. I had the opportunity to interview the legendary engineer Steve Wozniak (the co-founder of Apple) recently. It was a treat to speak with this living legend who has so impacted the world around him. Imagine what the world would be like without Apple?

Engineers want to know every detail about a project, which sometimes slows down the learning curve when they get involved in a new industry. But here's the good news about that: Once they learn a concept and believe in it, their conviction makes them want to teach it to everyone. Over the years, I've seen many engineers build massive agencies in the life insurance business.

10. Life Insurance Agents

The inclusion of this group may be a surprise to many of you because we don't often think of a life insurance agent as a hero. When I left the military, I had a decision to make about a career choice. A mentor suggested life insurance. He was an ex-Navy Seal who had done very well building several successful companies, so I valued his guidance. He told me that working in life insurance was one of the most rewarding jobs I can choose. I didn't understand what he meant by that until I started working in the field. The stories of many whose life insurance policies provided financial stability during a time of sorrow, eventually showed me the honor in helping others to be prepared for the inevitable.

After I gave a talk to a few hundred people on the topic of honorable professions, a lady approached me with tears in her eyes and told me she agreed that being a soldier and life insurance agent were both honorable and important. She then told me the story of her son, a soldier who had been killed in battle in Iraq. Her son had always wanted to be a soldier, knowing that it was dangerous. Before he died, her son had secretly purchased an additional life insurance policy for his family on top of what the military provides. This mom, who had lost so much, carried with her the pride in both her son's sacrifice for his country and in his effort to ensure that his family would be assisted in the event of his death.

How to Get Involved in the Life Insurance Industry

The word is starting to spread about the boom that is about to take place in the life insurance industry, which is attracting a variety of people. People are getting involved in the life insurance business for many reasons, and whatever their reasons may be, the business is flexible enough to suite the varied needs of each interested individual.

Here are four reasons why agents get involved in the insurance business part time:

> "Education is the most powerful weapon which you can use to change the world."
>
> — Mandela

I. The opportunity to learn how money works.

One of the reasons why I initially got involved in the financial industry was to simply learn the secrets of money. I think about the hundreds of thousands of people in America who are in the midst of challenging times financially because of the simple lack of fiscal education. Imagine if you were a construction worker building pools on a daily basis. What would you get very good at? Building pools. What if one day you and your family decided to build a pool in your own backyard—who would build it for you? You would, since that's what you do on a daily basis. What if you were a hair stylist and your son needed a haircut? Who would you trust to cut his hair? Probably yourself. How about if you were in the financial industry, where every day you educate others on how money works? Who would manage your own finances for you? You would. And ask yourself this: Would you ever take advantage of yourself financially? No, of course not, because that would be foolish. The point I'm making here is that the only way you'll fully feel comfortable about your own finances is by getting involved and learning how money works.

"If you stop learning, you will forget what you already know."

— Proverbs 19:27

2. The chance to earn part-time second income.

We're living at a time in which most people's primary income is not keeping up with inflation. I meet a lot of people who earn a six-figure income, who realize it no longer means what it used to in the '80s. Today, earning a low six-figure income really means you're only taking home somewhere around $5,000 to $6,000 a month, depending on the state and tax bracket you are in. The cost of college education is rising rapidly, which is a concern for parents who have children getting ready to enter college. How will these parents afford to fund their children's education, as well as their own retirement?

There are typically two different kinds of part-time agents in the industry. There are those who are part time with no plans of ever going full time because they love their full-time jobs. Some of them are in the military, others are police officers, teachers, nurses, or coaches; but they don't want to give their main career up, which they don't have to do unless they want to go full time in the life insurance industry. The second kind of part-time agents are those who are not happy with their full-time jobs but can't stop working because they need the income from their first job. But here's the good news: By getting involved in the insurance business part time, they build up their book of business and can eventually go full time and quit the job they dislike. In the case of either part-time agent, the life insurance business provides both job satisfaction and the flexibility to provide financially for your family.

3. A way to gain a competitive edge.

The life insurance business is starting to attract a higher number of professionals, such as attorneys and CPAs who are discovering the importance of having an edge in their business—and that edge is offering insurance to their clients as well as their usual services. Many of the professionals are also starting to see the bigger picture of recruiting and building an agency. I once spoke to a group of three hundred professional CPAs in Denver who were all getting their insurance license to provide an additional service to their clients. There were several CPAs in the room who were earning in the range of $250,000 and up, just from the additional financial and insurance side of their business. This doesn't mean everyone will earn this kind of extra income, but the opportunity certainly exists for such professionals.

4. A path to escape boredom and rediscover life's excitement.

> "The more you lose yourself in something bigger than yourself, the more energy you will have."
>
> — Norman Vincent Peale

When I speak to various people across the country, I often hear individuals say they need some spice in their lives. Their job has just become boring, offering very little in the way of purpose. The job is just something that they do on a daily basis and lacks the sense that there's a bigger cause behind it. Many are looking for a challenge to really test their limits and find out what they really have inside.

Too often people don't fully realize their capacity unless they put themselves in a position to see what they're really made of. It will always be a mystery to them what they could have done with their lives. At some point, we all realize that deep down inside we want to be counted on. I'm a firm believer in the fact that we were created to serve and be depended on. We do better when we're put in situations that require us to step up, and moreover we feel a certain void when no one relies on us. We start questioning our own worth. The insurance industry reaffirms your personal value and gives you a sense of pride in what you do because without your professional involvement, a family you helped could've been left behind not knowing how money works. This business is extremely rewarding and offers a certain sense of satisfaction that words can't describe.

There are several factors to look for when deciding to get involved in the life insurance business. The key is to know your choices and what you're looking to do personally. There are three ways in which you can get involved in the life insurance industry:

1. Part-time agent supplementing your full-time job.
2. A full-time producer selling life insurance and annuities.
3. A full-time broker building your own agency.

All three are excellent choices. Yours should be determined by what fits your life best.

Eight Points For YOU to Consider on How to Start Your Career

1. Choose a company that allows you to build your own agency within an agency.

I've covered many different points in this book, but the key point is that the biggest opportunity in the life insurance industry currently exists for those who decide to build their own agency. The timing couldn't be better to recruit and develop new agents, which provides the opportunity to earn an override as a broker. This allows you to earn income for the time you put into training the new agent. This not only gives you the highest potential for income, but it is also a stable, long-term business that you can count on to provide you freedom as a business owner.

2. Seek out opportunity for ownership.

One of the first clients I decided to go meet when I first started working at Morgan Stanley was a gentleman named Aaron who owned a windows company. He was a self-made millionaire who came to New York from Russia and had done extremely well in business. Since my good friend at the time was his assistant, she was able to set up a time for us to have an official business meeting. I gave him my business card and told him I had begun my career as an advisor and was interested in earning his business. He immediately asked me if I ever intended to be wealthy. I answered yes, and that's when he explained the concept of creating wealth in a way that no one else ever had before. He encouraged me to never work for a sexy, established company. When I asked why not, he simply said that an established company had a group of people who helped establish the company, and in the process they were given the opportunity to own a piece of the company. With the company established, those original founders are now wealthy. But at this point, I would just be an employee working for the firm. He challenged me to make the tough decision to go to a newer firm and help them become established, which would earn me the opportunity of one day owning a piece of the company and truly experiencing wealth. This is why I highly suggest that you go to a company where you not only have the chance to own your own book of business, but also eventually a piece of the life insurance agency itself. The key is that you're going to work hard building your business anyway, so why not put yourself in a position to maximize the return for your time?

3. Look for companies that Millennials are involved in.

Having Millennials involved in a company's leadership ensures that there is someone constantly doing what needs to be done to adapt to current times. We're living at a time when things are changing every single day. I was in line to buy an iPhone 4s when a lady in front of me turned around and said that I could always order the phone online and it would arrive in four weeks on my doorstep. I told her that I couldn't wait that long because by then the iPhone 5 would be coming out. I'm sure that you understand my humor, but the point is that things are changing very quickly. You want to make sure that there are people involved in the company who will stop at nothing in their quest for success. Millennials, with their desire to do the impossible and change the world, provide an enormous boost to a company when in leadership positions.

4. Look for multiple-provider carriers.

The internet has made a variety of information available to consumers, which means it has become difficult to sell expensive term-life insurance. It was easier in the '80s during the phase of "buy term and invest the difference," but today is a different era. Clients are purchasing a term policy, then immediately afterwards they are going online and realizing that there's a policy out there 40% cheaper than what they paid. This has caused more agents to see the value of offering multiple carriers, which allows them to compare policies based on the client's needs. It is not necessary to offer every single carrier, but I recommend having somewhere around three to five carriers that help your clients in the decision-making process.

5. Find a training program that offers you a personal mentor.

The great thing about the life insurance industry is that most companies offer initial training. But the challenge is that you are eventually left alone to figure out the intricacies of the field all by yourself. The best systems are those that offer a mentor for you to get started with, someone you can call on for answers to questions you don't yet have. One of the key benefits of having a good personal mentor is that the majority of them are all big believers in personal development. The insurance business has a track record of attracting and developing strong leaders who in turn develop others.

6. Don't overlook incentive trips!

If you choose the right opportunity, chances are you will have the added luxury of traveling all over the world. There are a lot of nice places to visit in the world, and I highly encourage you to do whatever you can to qualify for every trip. It's nice to travel the world, but it's even nicer when the company pays for everything.

7. Find a strategic compensation plan.

I often have people tell me what a high percentage they make on policies they write, but when I ask them about the income they make, they avoid the issue. The fact is, having a high percentage on policies doesn't guarantee you a high income when you're left alone to build an agency, or book of business by yourself. Remember, 90% of nothing is still nothing. I would suggest instead to seek out opportunities where you can work your way up with the firm while being trained properly. If you're taking the route of becoming a broker, it is also very important to find a compensation plan that rewards you for the leaders you develop.

> "People rarely succeed unless they're having fun in what they are doing."
>
> — Dale Carnegie

8. Run with a fun and innovative group of people.

After being in the workforce for a while, you realize you're going to spend more time with the people you work with than your own family. You may as well have fun with the people you work with on a daily basis. It's always great to work with a fun and innovative group of people because they bring out a side of you that wouldn't come out unless you were surrounded by people like them. I highly suggest you meet different leaders in the company you choose to work with to get an idea of what makes them different than their competitors.

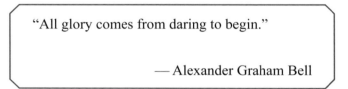

"All glory comes from daring to begin."

— Alexander Graham Bell

As you're finishing up this book, the good news is that the boom has just begun. My hope is for you to take the initiative to do your due diligence of finding an insurance company that's a good fit for you. There are many great leaders in the insurance business who are willing to take you under their wings and teach you the business as long as you're serious and committed to learning. It could possibly be one of the best business decisions you ever make in your life.

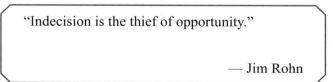

"Indecision is the thief of opportunity."

— Jim Rohn

This book has not only been about the life insurance business, it's also been about finding leaders who have the courage to at least give the industry a try. If you choose this industry at the very least, you will learn about different financial concepts, and knowledge that will serve you throughout your life. Alternatively, the best thing that could happen is that you find an industry that allows you to build the kind of a life you've always dreamt of building.

I'm also here to tell you that the first two years are going to be annoying at times, just like in any other business you get involved in. But if you're tough, strong, kind, caring, willing to work hard, and dedicated, there's no limit to how big you can build your empire. You could end up being the next success story being talked about in the industry.

> "Good things come to those who wait but only the things left behind by those who hustled."
>
> — Abe Lincoln

The conditions discussed in this book can help you capitalize on the perfect storm that is currently taking place. If you're someone who is serious about building an agency within the industry, I highly suggest you share this message with the people you know who would also have the desire to participate in this movement. Meanwhile, I invite you to stay in contact with me through my social media channels.

For more information on *The Next Perfect Storm*, you can follow Patrick Bet-David on Twitter, Facebook, or visit his website at www.patrickbetdavid.com. You may also contact his support team via e-mail at info@thenextperfectstorm.com.

References

Page 27
* http://corporate.mattel.com/about-us/history/default.aspx
* http://www.ideafinder.com/history/inventions/barbiedoll.htm

Page 28
* http://nces.ed.gov/pubs99/1999048.pdf

Page 29
* http://www.topspeed.com/cars/ford/1964-2006-ford-mustang-history-ar7823.html
* http://www.topspeed.com/cars/pontiac/1964-2003-pontiac-gto-history-ar7261.htmlhttp://www.topspeed.com/cars/chevrolet/1968-2002-chevrolet-camaro-history-ar1399.html
* http://www.musclecarclub.com/musclecars/pontiac-firebird/pontiac-firebird-history-1.shtmlhttp://www.edmunds.com/dodge/charger/history.html

Page 32
* http://www.irs.gov/retirement/article/0,,id=108950,00.html (Pension funds stats)
* http://www.getinvolved.gov/newsroom/programs/factsheet_boomers.asp
* (Baby Boomer facts)
* http://www.time.com/time/magazine/article/0,9171,1929233,00.html (Stats for the Time Magazine article.)

Page 34
* 1-Investopedia (http://www.investopedia.com/articles/mutualfund/05/MFhistory.asp#axzz1hxqb2iLS)
* 2-Wikipedia (http://en.wikipedia.org/wiki/History_of_banking#Emergence_of_merchant_banks)
* 3-http://en.wikipedia.org/wiki/Life_insurance#Annuities
* 4-Wikipedia (http://en.wikipedia.org/wiki/Lottery)
* 5-advisorworld 1/16/10 http://www.advisorworld.com/2010/01/3/annuities-friend-or-foe
* 6- advisorworld 1/16/10 http://www.advisorworld.com/2010/01/3/annuities-friend-or-foe
* 7- "The Early History of Annuity" by Edwin W. Kopf - An annuity is an investment you make through an insurance company that provides tax-deferred growth, guarantees, safety, death benefit, flexibility and the option of having monthly stream of income that you cannot outlive. Equity-indexed annuities provide you with participation in the stock market without any downside risk. Annuities guarantees are backed by the financial strength and claims paying ability of issuing insurance company. Some income and benefit features on an annuity may be offered at an additional cost in the form of a rider.

Page 36
* http://www.theripa.com/articles/historyannuities.pdf

Page 37
* http://www.bc.edu/bc_org/rvp/pubaf/06/Panel.pdf

Page 42
- http://www.fdic.gov/bank/individual/failed/banklist.html

Page 44
- http://moneyover55.about.com/od/howtoinvest/a/marketreturns.htm

Page 47
- http://www.freeby50.com/2008/05/more-on-historical-home-appreciation.html

Page 51
- http://en.wikipedia.org/wiki/Mutual_fund#History | http://www.vanguard.com/bogle_site/bogle_bio.html

Page 52
- http://online.wsj.com/article/SB10001424052748703954904575110163185399210.html

Page 59
- http://espn.go.com/nfl/playoffs/2011/story/_/id/7544243/super-bowl-2012-commercials-cost-average-35m

Page 66
- http://www.bls.gov/web/laus/lauhsthl.htm
- Infoplease.comhttp://www.infoplease.com/ipa/A0104719.html#ixzz1rhePJjH3

Page 81
- http://www.limra.com/newscenter/pressmaterials/11FOL.pdf

Page 83
- http://www.autoinsurance.org/when-did-auto-insurance-become-mandatory/

Page 84
- http://www.lifehappens.org

DOING THE
IMPOSSIBLE
The 25 Laws for Doing the Impossible
Patrick Bet-David

Remember when you were young and dreamed of doing the impossible? Becoming an NBA star? Traveling the world? Being the next great fashion designer? Starting the next iconic American company? Whatever your dream was as a child, chances are somewhere along the way that dream got lost in the nine-to-five grind, forgotten in the adult ideas of what is and what is not achievable.

Ask yourself this: If other people have overcome great odds, the doubts of others, and huge challenges to achieve the impossible, why not you? This book is a step-by-step guide to first becoming an impossibility thinker and then an impossibility doer.

Recreate Yourself.
If you are not happy with where you are in life today, the good news is that your path is not written in stone. This book will show you how to write your own story by recreating yourself as someone who can and will do the impossible.

Identify Your Cause.
This book is a roadmap for those who want to do something big with their lives. What lies at the end of that journey will be different for every individual. But one thing is true for all those looking to do the impossible: You must have a cause that captures your heart. The impossible is only possible if your cause is more powerful than the challenges that you will face along the way.

Go Make History.
This part of the roadmap will have mountains to climb and landmines to avoid, but at the end of the journey lies unfathomable rewards for your perseverance. When you reach the end, how will your family and friends describe you? What will the history books say about you? How will it feel to have done the impossible?

@DoingTheImpossibleBook

Recreate Yourself

Identify Your Cause

amazon.com.

Be sure to post your reviews on Amazon

Go Make History

BARNES&NOBLE
BOOKSELLERS

KEEP UP WITH PATRICK BET-DAVID

@patrickbetdavid

@patrickbetdavid

www.patrickbetdavidblog.com

www.patrickbetdavid.com